KENJU

The Art of
Japanese Swordsmanship

Acknowledgements

Thanks to Chadwick Minge for providing some of the black and white photographs.

ISBN: 0-86568-148-1
Library of Congress No. 89-50825

Designer: Danilo J. Silverio
Editor: John Steven Soet

**UNIQUE
PUBLICATIONS**
4201 Vanowen Place
Burbank, CA 91505

Dedication

For Jason,

The spirit can overcome the body only because of the heart.

Table of Contents

The Japanese Sword

Few weapons have the mystique of the Japanese sword. Forged under rites that are directly connected to Japan's Shinto religion, and labeled the "Soul of the Samurai," the Japanese sword serves as both a weapon and a work of art.

For hundreds of years, the sword also served as a symbol of rank. According to legend, the swordsmith Amakuni created the first true Japanese sword sometime around 700 A.D. Although there were small changes in blade design over the next thousand years, the actual shape of the weapon has changed little since it was invented. As a general term, the word *Katana* is used to mean Japanese sword, even though the swords themselves did vary in terms of length and weight.

The actual shape of the Katana must have been a solution to a number of problems.

Probably the most overlooked influence on the invention of the Katana is the type of sword technique used while riding a horse. Long before Amakuni, the Japanese had learned the art of (and advantages) fighting on horseback. The earlier straight thrusting swords used by the Japanese were okay for fighting on foot, but such swords are almost useless when one is on a horse. Any sword that is to be used in this fashion must be capable of a strong cutting motion because it is very difficult to make a good sword thrust while riding a fast horse. It should be remembered that a sword cut uses the arms while a sword thrust is really made with the legs (the arm just holds the sword in place while the legs provide the power). Obviously, when one is fighting on horseback, the ability to use footwork is limited. For horseback style fighting, the Katana is almost a perfect weapon.

Another need the Katana filled was that of a weapon that could be used against several opponents at the same time and against a wide variety of weapons. Few weapons can be used in such a wide variety of situations as a Katana.

Finally, the Katana is an extremely sharp sword. This might seem obvious, but in fact there are a number of sword types that are not all that sharp. The saber of the form used by the English in the 18th and 19th centuries was an example of a combat sword that did not have a remarkably sharp edge. However, since the Katana was used both against armored and unarmored opponents, it had a very keen edge.

Over the centuries, the size of the Katana has changed according to fashion and need. On the battlefield, a large Katana, called a *Daito*, or the slightly smaller *Tachi* was used. These swords could be as long as five feet and were used to cut down horses (and their riders) as well as a few enemy soldiers with one cut. Of course, such swords were not worn in the everyday world, and after the beginning of the Edo period, c. 1600, the shorter Katana proper came into fashion. An average length for a Katana is about 28 inches from hand guard to tip. A sword shorter than 24 inches measured in the same fashion is generally called a *Chisa-Katana*. Those under 18 inches are called *Wakizashi*. These weapons are followed by a variety of daggers that could be used for combat or serve as signs of rank.

The construction of the Japanese sword was done by layering of steel of various hardnesses together to produce a sword with a very hard edge and softer shock-resistant sword body. The process is complicated and varied. To the Japanese, often the proper "spiritual" preparation of the swordsmith is just as important as the smith's forging skills. As to whether this had any real influence on the sword itself is rather a moot point, but it did play an important role in sword construction.

Sword Training

Across cultures and historical periods, the sword has served as a symbol of office and authority. Even today, many elite military units wear swords when on dress parade. Oddly, even though a number of cultures have held the sword in high esteem, few have produced an advanced practice of swordsmanship. Such cultures as the Romans and the Vikings have left the names of few swordsmen and very little of their techniques and training methods. Even the European knights were not particularly famous for their sword technique. It was not until the 16th century that European swordsmanship really developed into something approaching scientific. At about this same time, Japanese sword technique began its great climb to maturity. This parallel development is very interesting because in the author's (sometimes unpopular) opinion, these two cultures went on to produce the finest swordsmen of any time and any place. Interestingly, the training methods of these two centers were and are very similar. Here, the Japanese approach to training will be explained. As noted earlier, this training is used to train in the *combative* use of the sword.

The word *combative* is very important. Such sports as kendo and foil fencing are good training, but are fundamentally different from training intended for life-and-death struggles. Such sports are interesting but they do not train one how to approach facing a live blade without fear or self-consciousness. Without this attitude, one would almost be better off not having any training. Why? Because such sports, with their overemphasis on scoring points, often leave the individual with an overly aggressive attitude. This often leads to the habit of attacking constantly without any judgment of the situation. To prevent the development of such bad (in other words, fatal) habits, the sword masters of Japan created a comprehensive training program. Contrary to popular opinion, kata training was not all there was to training.

Before kata training could be started, certain basics had to be learned and practiced. Stretching, basic footwork and solo training with heavy weighted swords would be central to this training. This training with wooden swords is called *suburei*, and is the basis for the swordsman's cutting power. In addition to suburei, actual cutting was practiced on a variety of targets ranging from human bodies (usually executed criminals) to animals, to specially constructed targets.

This is probably the most overlooked skill in such sports as kendo or fencing. In kendo, the stress is on hitting (sliding cuts don't count). In fencing, points are often scored with a "curved thrust," which rarely has the sword's length or the fencer's weight behind it. Just hitting with the best of swords will not produce a telling cut, and a thrust that does not travel in a straight line will not penetrate.

Suburei, cutting (*tamashigiri*) and basic conditioning is fairly standard from sword style to sword style. It is in the kata of the various schools that the real difference can be seen today. It should be mentioned that in all probability, the early kata were more of the one step or one attack and counter type. The written records of the Yagyu family and Miyamoto Musashi describe techniques that are comprised of one, two or at most three movements. These early techniques were practiced at real combat intervals, which precluded a long, drawn out sequence. The longer sequences also have much to offer, but some explanation is needed if one is to understand their value.

The long sequences of techniques generally referred to as kata are generally performed at a distance of about half-a-step out of real combat distance. This makes it possible to string together a series of techniques so as to form a long two-man sword dance. If one were to practice just these series without the shorter one-step training and the cutting training mentioned earlier, then they would have some very real difficulties when faced with an opponent who wants to fight at a distance other than the half-step-out mentioned earlier. One of the chief advantages of the long kata training is that it effectively programs the swordsman's reflexes, which in turn makes him far faster than someone not so trained. Another advantage of this training is that it is a very good device for memorizing a large number of techniques.

Once the series of techniques has been learned, the instructor will change the order or switch to a different sequence entirely. These actions are designed to check the level at which a trainee understands and can use the techniques within the longer series.

The kata used in classical kenjutsu have another side effect that is often overlooked. It is very good exercise, which helps the swordsman maintain a high level of conditioning.

On the mental level, kata training is directed at teaching the proper mental attitude for combat. Training with hard wood swords or even live blades carries with it a given level of danger. Without proper instruction, the all-important element of judgment will not be learned or, worse yet, misunderstood.

The sad sight of World War II Japanese officer charging machine guns is an example of what can happen when proper judgment is not learned. While in some parts of the world this type of action may be considered courageous, it is, in the final analysis stupid. Why? Because losing a sense of oneself is in reality a technique one uses so as to have the best chance of winning, not to knowingly throw away one's life with no possible gain, except perhaps that of the enemy.

Kenjutsu and Japanese Martial Arts

When one looks at the wide variety of Japanese martial arts, it is at first very difficult to find a common denominator in them. However, on closer examination, some elements can be found. One of the most important is the role played by the sword.

In the classical martial arts, no other weapon held the status of the sword. It was the center of training. This was because this weapon was carried by all warriors as their right. All of the kata of the older schools have the sword as the central element. Thus when learning the techniques of spear or staff, these were first learned against the sword. Later, such arts as jujutsu were designed with defense against a sword as central idea to their techniques. Even the later arts of judo and aikido are influenced by the sword. Advanced judoka practice forms of defense against the sword in kata that spring from older jujutsu schools. In aikido, the entire art shows a very strong influence of swordsmanship. Even the esoteric art of ninjutsu was influenced by the ever present Japanese sword. It is interesting to note that many people training in martial arts that have been influenced by the sword do not even know how to hold that weapon.

It has been supposed that the art of swordsmanship has lost much of its value as a martial because the sword is no longer used as a weapon. While there may be some truth in this idea, it is in reality argument of the simple minded. In terms of skill, few weapons come close to the demands of swordsmanship. Also, through the art of iaido (the art of sword drawing), the philosophy of martial arts can be approached. As far as the actual practical value of training with a sword, it should be remembered that swords move much faster than the fastest human hand or foot and judgment learned through sword training will carry over to all other skill areas.

The evolution of kendo from kenjutsu is interesting, and given the evolution of combat to sport, it was more or less certain. With the rise of peace after 1600, the chances to test one's skill with a sword were rather rare. Of course duels did take place, but as time passed, these duels came to be the exception.

Added to this was the rise of the power of the merchant class as commerce became more important. Like merchants of other countries, this class had the wish to better its social status, and thus adopted many of the habits of what it saw as its social superiors. Because of its central position, the art of sword was one such area that received much attention.

As to whether paladins are made or born the author will not comment. However, few of the members of the merchant class that bought their way into the rank of swordsman were prepared to face the discipline or had the mental make up of the classical warrior.

This sort of situation led to changes in kenjutsu. Sometime after 1700 the shinai (split bamboo sword) was developed. According to many sources, the swordsman Nakanishi Chuzo developed this sword in 1750 so as to prevent injuries in practice. It should be noted that as early as c. 1600 the Yagyu Shinkage ryu used a similar idea to train their swordsmen. So in reality, the formation of kendo was a natural outgrowth of earlier development.

In any case, the use of protective equipment along with a "safe" weapon made the rise of a sporting form of sword possible. (This same evolution took place in Europe and ended in the formation of modern fencing.) Along with the change in equipment, came the need for rules and this change the character of the type of swordsmanship practiced.

The differences in kenjutsu and kendo are interesting and a few should be mentioned. In kendo, the targets are the head, wrist, body and, to a lesser extent, the throat. In kenjutsu, any part of the body can be cut. The targets in kenjutsu often had to take the opponent's armor into account. Thus, some of the targets for a sword attack (when an opponent wore armor) were the inside of the wrist, inside of the thighs, waist, thumb and eyes. These spots were often covered by no armor or were at the joints in that armor. The need for considering the presence of armor means that today, when one sees a technique of one of the ko-ryu (classical schools), they must remember that the technique practiced may in fact be intended for use against an armor-clad opponent. Thus, it is unfair to judge kenjutsu by totally modern standards. Another element that is important in these two arts is the differences in weapons used. Of course, in kendo the sword is used either against other swords, or in some cases against two swords. In kenjutsu, such a wide variety of weapons as spears, staffs and halberds were used. However, in kenjutsu, the sword was (and is) the central weapon.

Famous Swordsmen

Japan's martial arts are filled with the tales of single swordsmen fighting and defeating vastly superior numbers. These tales are for the most part just that — tales. However, there is some basis for these myths. The famous swordsmen Ittosai, Yagyu, and Musashi all at one time faced several opponents and managed to survive the encounters. This, combined with the dueling record of a particular individual, is what makes these swordsmen remembered as the best in Japan's history.

In spite of vastly different life styles (Musashi was a lone wolf, while the Yagyu family was deeply involved in politics) all of these swordsmen had elements of their life that were common.

Almost all of them lived their lives by the sword, and in spite of battles or duels, still died of natural causes. At that time, life was really not worth much, and anyone following the Way of the sword could not realistically expect to live to an old age. Most did not.

The four men included in this short section killed quite a number of fellow swordsmen. All of these men founded their own sword styles and, in reality, their own martial arts. They all spent time wandering the country looking for opponents with whom to improve their skills. All of them left written records of their approaches to the sword, although in Ittosai's case this written record was in the form of a scroll left to a student after he retired.

It is interesting to note that none of these men never left Japan and, with the exception of Ittosai, they never faced a martial artist from another country. This is one of those events in history that unquestionably helped boost the overall image of the Japanese sword technique.

It also has been written that Musashi may have learned the rapier and dagger technique of the Europeans who traded and sailed around southern Japan. This is interesting because the Europeans have historically used a one-handed sword technique, whereas this technique did not really have a following in Japan until after Musashi.

One-handed attacks have a natural reach advantage over two-handed attacks because, when using only one hand, it is possible to turn the body so as to face the opponent sideways. When using both hands, the body stands directly at the opponent. While it has never been proven that Musashi did in fact learn the European technique, it is a rather strange occurrence in the history of Japanese swordsmanship, and it should be remembered that in the case of Musashi, a lot of things cannot be proven from historical papers.

The written records of Japanese sword schools are almost never questioned, but it is the author's contention that even old written records must not be accepted at face value. Almost all the written records of Japan's sword schools have been "passed down," and are to this day accepted without question. Considering Japan's rather damp climate, unquestionably more records have been lost than what is available today. Often such scrolls had to be recopied with the facts sometimes adjusted to fit the interest of the school doing the actual writing. Very few sword schools have records that can be proven to date from the actual founding of the school, and even this is not always an indication that the school lives up to the founder's level of skill.

Therefore, the following short outlines of some of Japan's famous swordsmen should be read with the thought that what is contained in them is based on the available information, and that some events which cannot be historically confirmed with some certainty are left out.

It should be noted that there are many famous swordsmen who are left out. The roles of the Yagyu and Itto ryu could easily fill a book. What is presented here is a brief outline of the most famous men, and a short description of the methods that were special to their approach to the sword. It should be noted that the schools of today will often have elements of other schools' techniques. This is only natural, as each school adopted what was useful and practical and discarded that which was not. The association of the Yagyu and Itto ryu (through the Shogun) must have resulted in some cross instruction as the two schools coexisted over the years.

Oddly enough, there is no record of any of the men in this section ever having crossed swords. There is a story about Musashi meeting and training for a short time under Ittosai, but this is probably just an attempt by mainstream schools to explain that man's extraordinary skill. It should be noted that he met men from just about every major school, and made short work of all of them.

It is, of course, impossible to pass judgment on who had the most skill with a sword. Members of the Itto ryu would certainly answer that question differently than a Yagyu ryu man.

From the facts given, the readers can decide for themselves.

Tsukahara Bokuden

Born in December 1490, in Kashima, Hitachi province. Although not as well-known in the West as some of Japan's other swordsmen, Bokuden left a record of duels and battles that was probably never matched. According to oral tradition, he fought in over 30 battles, and between 20 and 30 duels using steel swords. Trained from an early age in the sword styles of the Kashima and Shinto, Bokuden began his life as a wandering swordsman during his teens. Before he died at the age of 81, he was given credit for having dispatched over 200 enemies.

The sword school known as the Kashima style is supposed to have been founded by him. Many of the techniques of this school have similarities with those of the Shinto style. One of the main ideas of the Kashima style is that idea of *hitotsu-tachi*. This idea is based on the concept of "one cut" or "one stroke."

While this concept is fairly difficult for someone not trained in classical bujutsu to understand in application, the idea is easy to explain in print. Concisely, this idea calls for a swordsman to wait to the very last instant before he counters an opponent's attack. If done correctly, the opponent's weapon will miss by less than an inch. Added to this is the realization that different parts of a sword have different cutting power. Thus, the last one-third of a sword has the most power, while the middle third has less and the last third has almost none at all. In fact if one steps straight into a cut, he can often be struck by the last third of a sword blade without being injured. This, of course, takes proper training, but it is possible.

Yagyu Muneyoshi

With Yagyu, swordsmanship reached a new level. Born in the year 1529, Yagyu was destined to bring changes to the martial arts that would exert influences down to the present day.

At a fairly early age, Yagyu began his career as a swordsman by fighting in battles. Later, Yagyu began to wander Japan in an effort to perfect his technique. During these wanderings, he met Kamiizumi Hidetsuna, who was an expert of the Kage ryu. Yagyu became Kamiizumi's student and later the leader of the style of marital art known as the Shinkage ryu. Still later, Yagyu made an extensive study of all of the major styles of his day and founded the Yagyu Shinkage ryu based on his efforts.

In the year 1594, Yagyu became the teacher and tutor of Tokugawa Ieyasu, who in 1603 would become Shogun and, in effect, the head of the Japanese government. Thus through Yagyu, the philosophies of swordsmanship and Zen had a very real influence on the government of Japan.

It should be noted that Yagyu was a major influence in introducing the influence of Zen into the martial arts and sword technique in particular. Yagyu's son Munenori and his grandson Mitsuoshi were also famous for their sword technique.

When one reads Yagyu's *Heiho Kaden Sho*, they can get a glimpse of his style. Often it would appear that he devised counters for favorite techniques of other schools active in his lifetime. However, the amount of study needed to do this is vast. One of the special techniques of the Yagyu ryu is *muto*, or no sword. With these techniques, it is possible for an unarmed man to defeat a sword-armed opponent. The level of skill required to do this is one very good indication of Yagyu's skill.

Miyamoto Musashi

Of all the famous swordsmen in the pages of Japanese history, none has quite the reputation (both good and bad) of Musashi. Born in 1584, in the village of Miyamoto, Musashi's life would be one long story of one man's efforts to master the way of the sword. Beginning at the age of 13, when he fought and killed Arima Kibei (by beating him to death with a staff) Musashi's life was marked by duels, battles and constant wandering.

Unlike most famous swordsmen, Musashi did not belong to any particular school. Much of his training was probably learned from his father while he was a young child. During the course of his duels, Musashi made use of just about anything to win.

Not only did he use such oddball weapons as boat oars, fence posts and throwing knives, he also used a great deal of what today would be called psychological warfare. Often he would arrive late for duels (a very serious insult in Japan), and he collected as much information on his opponent beforehand as possible. While such tricks may be frowned upon by many, it should be noted that in spite of a life marked by duels and battles, Musashi did die of natural causes at the age of 61.

Musashi is remembered as the founder of the two-sword or *nito* method of fencing. While this idea had been used before Musashi, he perfected the idea. There is a general misunderstanding about his system. Nito is based on the ability to fence while holding a Japanese sword in one hand. Since tradition says that Musashi was over six feet tall (a giant by Japanese standards), this approach would have improved his reach advantage even more. Another important element in Musashi's approach is that through constant training, one should be able to wield a sword in one hand with the same dexterity as a pair of chopsticks. Thus, the idea of nito is more akin to having two swords used independently at the same time than that of two working together.

In addition to the skills mentioned above, Musashi's system was based on disrupting an opponent's rhythm so as to defeat him. According to remarks made in his book *Go Rin No Sho (A Book of Five Rings)*, his entire strategy is based on timing and rhythm.

Ito Ittosai

"Learn by being cut." This rather strange advice gives an example of this harsh swordsman's character. Unlike many sword experts of his day, Ittosai attached little mystical belief in swordsmanship or its techniques. Although not totally mechanical, the Itto ryu has the reputation of being one of the most technique oriented of the classical sword schools.

Ittosai received his formal training from Kanemaki Kanemaki of the Chujo ryu. After less than five years of training, Ittosai announced that he had reached a full understanding of the underlying principals of swordsmanship, then backed it up by defeating Kanemaki in a series of practice matches. He then began one of his many wandering trips to polish his techniques.

The main idea of the Itto ryu is that one technique can be expanded in a countless number. Central to Ittosai's idea of swordsmanship was that of the attitude of not losing. Instead of striving for victory, a swordsman (according to Ittosai) should concentrate on not losing. Proper timing and the training to be able to apply proper timing is critical to this idea. The key technique to the Itto ryu is *kiri-otoshi*. This could also be called an opposition cut because the technique itself makes a counter cut which deflects an attacker's cut, all in one motion. The advantage of timing this idea gives over an opponent has to be seen to be understood. Parry, counterattack and defeat of the opponent all take place in an instant in one stroke of a sword.

Sword Grip

The sword is held loosely, with the greatest strength in the little finger. There is a space between the hands as in photo (1). In the beginning of training, the trainee is often told to hold his sword with the index fingers held out as in (2) so as to develop the proper grip. The left hand should be next to the hand guard, which is also very close to the sword's center of balance (4). A common mistake is holding the sword with the hands together as in (5).

3

4

5

Continued

19

Stances (Kamae)

The number of sword stances have been recorded to be as high as 300 or possibly even more. While this may be true, it should be noted that in terms of function, many of these stances must have been identical. Also, in modern kendo, there are really only three or four stances that are used in the majority of matches. In terms of overall importance, the stances of upper, middle, lower, right and left deserve the most study.

Of these, the most important is *chudan no kamae* (1). Here, the entire length of the sword is placed between one's body and the opponent. This stance is used to make a straight thrust, push cuts and parries.

The next two stances, *gedan no kamae* (2) and *jodan no kamae* (3) are made by raising or lowering the sword point. Gedan no kamae is often used to make an upward counter cut to an opponent's hands as he attacks. Jodan no kamae is a very important stance and can be used in either attack or defense.

By bringing the sword to one's side with the point up, one makes *hasso no kamae* (4). This is a fairly neutral stance that is often overused (probably because it is similar in appearance to a baseball batting stance). If one brings the point back then they are standing in *waki no kamae* (5). This stance is often used to combine a retreat with a counter cut or a sidestep with a cut.

Two stances which are very useful in mixed-weapon situations, such as sword vs. spear, are *kasumi no kamae* (6) and *hiryu no kamae* (7). Both of these stances allow for very strong cuts after parries, as can be seen in the technique section. The *honguaku no kamae* stance is the mark of the Ona-ha Itto ryu (8). This stance is very descriptive in that there is a real opening for attack.

The *kongo no kamae* (9) is rather passive and has little to recommend it. The *yoko no kamae* (10) is often used by men of the Tenshin ryu. This stance can be used to evade and counter cut at the same time.

The *gyaku yoko no kamae* (11) and its many variations is favored by Yagyu swordsmen. Like yoko no kamae, this stance can be used for both attack and defense in one motion.

Stances (12-14) show variations of *chudan no kamae*. The kneeling stance (12) is useful at night when one wants to see an opponent against the skyline. The reinforced chudan no kamae (13) is good for reinforced parries. This technique is often used by the Katori and Kashima styles. Standing with the left foot forward in chudan no kamae give (14). In this stance the hands should be slightly back.

1

2

3

4

Continued

5

6

9

10

7

8

11

12

Continued

13

14

Nito Stances (Two Sword)

The use of two swords also created the need for stances that make movement easy. Although here too there are many possible stances, only a few need be illustrated. Standing with the swords crossed is probably one of the simplest and most functional of all of these (1). From this position, the X block is easy to apply in almost any direction.

Standing with the long sword held behind the body (2) is very similar to *waki no kamae,* where the swordsman will sidestep and whip his long sword around into the opponent or his weapon. Standing with the sword and scabbard crossed is useful if one has one hidden in or on the scabbard (3). If there is no such weapon, then this stance is dramatic, but that is about all. Standing with the long sword forward and the short sword covering the body (4) is also a good general stance that is, for all practical purposes, a form or chudan no kamae. Stances (5 & 6) show two examples of *shizen no kamae,* or natural stance. The natural stance represents a very high level of martial arts realization and should be studied deeply.

1

2

Continued

3

4

5

6

Continued

Distance and Timing

Few areas of martial arts require the level of skill in proper distance and timing control as sword technique. In unarmed fighting, a less-than-accurate response can result in receiving a glancing blow, but this is not always serious. The same mistake when facing a sword would result in a crippling wound.

It is true that an expert in martial arts is not so much a skillful "technique" man, but rather one who has mastered distance and timing. No matter how strong an attack is, if one is standing out of reach or out of line of the attack, then the attack's strength has no effect. Even fairly small men can control very large and strong opponents by using distance and timing properly.

A proper understanding of distance can make an opponent's attempts to use fakes totally useless. Instead or reacting, one has to only slightly adjust his distance to his opponent. Also, if the fake response is done properly, one will know the exact instance to strike through the fake and end the conflict.

The riddle of when to attack and when to counter is also a function of distance and timing. If one is standing at a distance close enough to the opponent, then he should strike without waiting. If one stands too far away then such an attack is easy to counter. Although there is no exact way to apply this idea because no two situations are exactly alike, for the purpose of explanation, a few guidelines can be given.

The critical distance in swordsmanship is when two opponents are standing at such a distance, so that the tips of their swords are touching. At this distance, the conflict will be decided in a flash. Long, drawn out blade clanging against blade duels are a creation of fiction. In real sword fighting, everything ends in one or two movements that can happen so fast that a witness might not even see what actually happened. Often, one swordsman will use a stance so that his sword is held in such a way that his opponent cannot touch his blade. This move is often done so that the complex techniques involving blade-on-blade play are not possible. Thus, one must be able to judge this blade-touching- blade distance even if he cannot see his opponent's blade because of the way he holds it.

When an opponent actually attacks, his attack must be avoided at the last possible instant by the least distance. If one were to take a piece of paper and write "life" on one side and "death" on the other, he could see the type of distance that is involved. In kenjutsu, the distance between life and death is the width of a piece of paper. In one famous duel, Musashi had a headband cut from his head yet he was not hurt. This type of distancing is totally different from the type used in sport martial arts. It is also a different timing. The appearance of being hit does not always mean that anything important has happened. In fact, it is better if the opponent thinks (if only for an instant) that his attack has worked. This will cause him to slacken his guard and thus present an opening.

This timing of waiting for the attack to almost reach the intended target before actually countering it is difficult to see when watching a *kumitachi* (two-man kata set) because of the speed of the motions and more importantly, the motions are set and can be practiced to a fairly high level of skill without ever really perfecting timing skills. Drills such as one-set kata (one attack) and one counter can help refine this skill.

The reason that proper timing is often not found in kumitachi is not that the method is faulty but rather that not all people understand the depth of the very method that they are practicing. Today, this is particularly the case because more and more people are learning from men who have not passed through the various levels of this type of training.

The area of study that is called distance and timing should not be thought of as two separate elements that stand alone. The distance at which men stand is really the beginning point and the timing is the process of them closing and doing their techniques. It should be noted that the distance will have a very real influence on the stance a swordsman can use. This in turn influences timing. For example, if a swordsman faces an opponent then the closer his opponent moves then he will have to make slight adjustments to his stance.

This is one of the main reasons that the middle posture (*chudan no kamae*) is considered the key stance is swordsmanship. That is, this stance is always correct regardless of the distance. While it is true that to strike from chudan no kamae one must sometimes raise the sword, this is not true in the art of sword in terms of real swords. It is possible to make many strong attacks from chudan no kamae without raising one's sword even one inch. For general purposes, the following guide can be used to help the reader understand the relationship of stance and distance (Note: this guide is for the general reader's information, a skilled swordsman can operate without ever having to use any stance whatsoever; however, this is because at a higher level, the swordsman becomes aware of what can be called "spiritual timing." But this is far above the purposes of this book). At a far distance, *hasso no kamae* and *waki no kamae* can be used. Slightly closer, *jodan no kamae* and *gedan no kamae* can be used.

Chudan no kamae can always be used. The reason for this guide's structure is the distance of the sword's cutting blade (or edge) from the opponent. This distance structure should be studied in practice to be really understood. In terms of distance and stance, some situations are classical and are often repeated in a variety of techniques. Thus, the situation of gedan no kamae against jodan no kamae is often seen. Hasso no kamae is often used against chudan no kamae. The match-ups probably stem from both swordsmen wanting to kill the opponent as quickly as possible (normally with one cut). Struggles that became wrestling matches were to be avoided if at all possible because while one was tangled with an opponent, it was possible for him to receive help and this could make life rather difficult and short for the swordsman trapped and outnumbered.

Mutual Slaying (ai uchi)

One of the greatest dangers facing an expert swordsman is that of mutual killing. The great founder of the Moto ryu, Yamaoka Tesshu once said that killing another person is not difficult *if* one is not concerned with his own life. This should always be remembered by swordsmen because any enemy who is totally unconcerned with his own safety is truly dangerous. This is often particularly the case when one is facing an injured opponent whose injury creates desperation. Two simple examples of ai uchi that illustrate this point can be seen in the following: The defender in (1), on the left stands in hasso no kamae and simply waits for the attack. When the opponent attacks, the defender doesn't move, but rather cuts with all his strength straight at the attacker (2). This, of course, results in mutual slaying. In a similar application, from (3), the attacker tries a straight thrust which is countered with a full-strength cut (4). It should be noted that in both cases the defender simply stood his ground and struck the opponent as soon as he stepped forward.

1

2

Continued

3

4

Simple Attacks

Simple attacks are attacks where the swordsman simply reaches around or over his opponent's blade to make an attack. Although "simple" in terms of motion, these attacks form the basis of just about all other motions. Often, it is good to practice these motions against a target that one can actually cut with a live blade (*tamashigiri*). Without such practice, the more complicated cuts will not work.

One of the most basic and important simple attacks is *men uchi*, or straight downward attack to the head. The power of this technique is hard for the untrained to understand. If done properly, this cut could split a human body down the middle with comparative ease. From (1), the attacker raises his sword (2), and then steps around the point of the opponent's blade to make the downward cut (3).

This same type of attack can be used against a variety of targets. From (4), the attacker uses a smaller motion to raise his sword (5), and cut the opponent's wrist (6).

1

Continued

2

3

4

5

6

Beat or Hitting Attacks

Often it is not possible to strike the opponent without first exerting some measure of control over his weapon. One of the most direct methods to do this is the beat attack to the opponent's sword. This is done hitting the opponent's blade and then striking home through the opening made by the attack on the opponent's blade. It should be noted that the best defense against such attacks is either simply to avoid the beat by moving one's weapon or simply taking a half-step backward or to the side so as to adjust the distance from the opponent.

It is only possible to use beats if the opponent is holding his weapon in such a fashion so that it can be reached fairly easily. From (1), the attacker brings his sword around (2) and then slightly up (3), so as to hit the opponent's weapon downward (4), and then thrust to the throat (5).

Often the beat attack takes the form of a push. From (6), the attacker uses a motion which is sort of a cross between a hit and push to misplace the opponent's sword (7). He then pushes his sword across the enemy's wrist (8).

When using beat attacks, it is important that the actual hitting not be done with the cutting edge of the sword. The back or flat of the sword should be used. From (9), the attacker steps around and hits his opponent's sword downward using the back of his sword blade (10). He then thrusts the sword up in the throat without changing the sword's angle (11).

Similar to the beat attack is taking control of the opponent's blade so as to create an opening. From (12), the attacker slides his own blade down the opponent's blade (13), then winds the sword around (14), to cut the opponent's neck (15). He then uses a quick spin to cut the body (16), and follows through (17), to cut the back (18). Such spinning cuts are very useful if one has to deal with a man in armor or more than one opponent.

1

2

3

4

Continued

5

6

7

8

9

10

Continued

11

12

13

14

15

16

Continued

17

18

Simple Counters

Simple counters are basic motions used to counter attacks. Generally, these motions combine a body movement that will clear one's body off the line of attack with a simple counter cut or thrust. In kenjutsu, the best way to counter an attack is to avoid it entirely and, in the same motion, make a powerful counter that will either kill the opponent instantly, or render him totally helpless. Not only does this end the conflict quickly, but it will also avoid broken weapons which are a sure source of embarrassment if one has to face more than one opponent. Along with simple attacks, these simple counters should be given the most attention in training.

One of the great advantages of chudan no kamae is that it makes a variety of simple counters possible. This is because this stance puts the entire length of the sword between oneself and the opponent. It also places the sword point closer to the opponent than any other stance. For example, from (1), the swordsman on the left raises his sword to attack, and the defender simply steps forward at a slight angle and cuts his wrist (2). In another example, the same attack is countered by leaving the sword where it is and simply stepping forward (3 & 4).

Some of the simple counters take advantage of the fact that as a swordsman finishes a cut there is a split second where he cannot really counter a cut. Thus, from (5), the attacker on the left uses a men uchi attack, the defender steps slightly back (6), and then forward to cut attacker's wrist (7). It is important that the counter cut is made at the instant that the attacker's hands stop. It is also possible to step to the side (8), and then counter.

Spins are often used to avoid the opponent's blade. From (9), the attack from the left is avoided with a spin (10), then a counter (11). Note that the countercut is done with a step so as to use the body's full weight behind it.

Classical kenjutsu was often performed on "the pass," which means that often two men fighting in this fashion would actually pass beside each other during the course of a fight. The pass is more important when one or both opponents are wearing armor because of the extra power needed to overcome such an opponent. Passes are one reason that kenjutsu has some of the spins often seen. As one passed the enemy, he would spin so as to make one, two or even three cuts to the opponent's body.

A simple but very important pass technique can be seen in the series. From (12), the attacker on the left uses men uchi. The defender runs past the attacker and in the same motion cuts his midsection (13). The cut is powerful and its follow-through brings the sword up so it can be used to make another forceful cut if needed (14).

Often it is possible to use pushing cuts to set up a pass. From (15), the attacker on the left makes a horizontal cut at the defender's body. The defender counters by stepping and sliding his sword across the attacker's hands (16). As he pushes, the defender spins the attacker around (17), so he can be finished with a cut across the back (18).

Another effective method of simple counters is that of diving under the opponent's technique. From a kneeling posture (19), the defender dives under the attacker's men uchi and drives his sword upward through the attacker's throat (20). The step forward can be done at a slight angle if needed (21).

Often, the stance a swordsman uses would indicate what technique he would use. From (22), the attacker on the left uses men uchi, the defender sidesteps and brings his sword down to cut the opponent's wrist (23). If the opponent raises his sword from (24), the defender brings his sword up to cut from underneath (25). During this technique, the defender's sword moves in a figure-eight pattern as it moves up and down.

1

2

3

4

5

Continued

6

7

8

9

10

11

Continued

12

13

14

15

16

17

Continued

18

19

20

21

22

23

Continued

24

25

Parrying Techniques

While it is most desirable that one counter an attack directly, without ever touching the opponent's sword, such is not always possible. Often the attack will be too quick or come at the end of a series of movements. This will make a simple counter impossible. In such cases, parries are needed. Parries are usually done with either the side or back of the blade. Also, the parry is done so as to deflect the attacking sword away rather than block it. A direct block will almost certainly result in a broken blade. Even the techniques that are called "reinforced blocks" are done at an angle that will allow the majority of the attacker's force to slide harmlessly off the blade.

One of the most important parrying techniques is shown in the series. This technique has the advantage of making a parry, and at the same time bringing the sword up so as to make a very powerful countercut. From (1), the attacker on the left uses men uchi. The defender sidesteps and raises his hands so that the opponent's sword slides downward (2). He then steps around and makes his counter (3).

Although not as powerful, the slapping parry is also very useful. From (4), the attacker on the left uses men uchi. The defender sidesteps to his left and pushes his sword to the right, thus forcing the attacking blade to the side and down (5). He then makes a quick cut to the attacker's throat (6).

The same motion that is used in the slapping parry can be used to combine a parry and a countercut in one motion. From (7), the attacker on the left uses men uchi, which the defender sidesteps. At the same instant he brings his sword around to cut the attacker's left hand and neck (8). He then slides his sword forward across both targets (9).

Dealing with horizontal cuts can be done in one of two basic fashions. The first technique would be used if the attack were at a lower portion of the body, while the second method would be used against higher attacks.

From (10), the attacker on the left makes a horizontal cut (*do giri*). The defender brings his sword around so that it meets the attacker's sword at an angle (11), and pushes the sword slightly downward, along the line of attack (12). He then turns and countercuts the attacker's midsection.

Against a high horizontal cut the same principle can be applied, but in an upward direction. From (14), the attacker cuts at the defender's neck. The defender ducks and brings his sword up at an angle (15), so that the attack slides up and around (16). He then cuts down the opponent's neck (17), and back (18).

Often when one thinks of classical kenjutsu, one forgets that the swordsmen of old Japan wore armor, and this had an influence on how techniques were done. In our example, one technique that would work under most circumstances is shown. It should be noted that Japanese armor does not usually provide heavy protection to the wearer's feet.

From (19), the attacker on the right uses men uchi, which is met with a fake parry, which turns into a direct cut to the attacker's foot (21-22). The same idea can be used with a direct thrust to the foot when combined with a *taiken* or body strike to the attacker's hands (23-24).

1

2

3

4

5

Continued

6

7

8

9

10

11

Continued

12

13

14

15

16

17

Continued

18

19

20

21

22

23

Continued

24

The next series shows how *kamae* (stance) is related to the parries or counters which can be used from a particular stance. In (1), the defender on the right used hiryu no kamae, while the attacker on the left uses jodan no kamae. The hiryu no kamae has many advantages but one of the most important is that one has to learn only two parries to use it. All attacks that come from above the right are parried as in series (1-3), and all attacks coming from the right are parried down as in (4-7).

From (1), the attacker uses men uchi, which the defender counters by stepping aside and raising his hands (2). As the attacker's sword slides by, the defender counters (3).

From (4), the attacker on the left uses a straight thrust which is countered by pushing down (5). The defender then punches the attacker's hands (6), and steps in for a countercut/throw combination (7).

1

Continued

5

6

7

Reinforced Blocks

Although technically not blocks, the techniques illustrated in this section are some of the most important in terms of actual Samurai combat. To understand this, one must remember a few things about the type of battlefield one finds when looking back into Japan's past. For the footsoldier, combat was usually done on a run or fast trot. This helped to increase the shock value of his attack and also help make him a less attractive target to the always-present archers. For the man on horseback the foot-work used to avoid an opponent's cut or thrust would be impossible. In fact, it is very difficult to create a special fencing system while mounted on a horse because of the lack of body movement possible on horseback. Therefore, simple blocks, attacks and counters are the order of the day.

The case of the footsoldier is probably more interesting because of the limitations placed on him by the type of combat used. When running, it is not possible to hold the sword hilt with both hands without slowing down one's pace. Also, the more complicated beat attacks would not be possible in that by the time one had actually hit the opponent's weapon, the opponent would have run by before a countercut could be made. Therefore, as one ran through the battlefield, he would hold the sword in one hand (usually the right), and as he approached an enemy he would either grab the hilt and attack with a simple cut or thrust, or place his hand on the back of the sword and deflect the opponent's attack so as to be able to have his blade slide by, then counter as the distance between them closed.

One of the chief advantages of placing one's hand on the sword's ridge line is the ease with which he can then make *atemi* (strikes) with the sword's hilt. From (1), the attacker raises his sword and makes a downward cut (2). The defender brings his sword up at an angle so that the attack slides by (3). He then steps inside and strikes the attacker's face with the sword hilt. This is followed by downward pressure to the attacker's arms so as to force him down (5). If the attacker had attacked on a run, the hilt blow would probably knock him senseless.

As with any type of technique, this hilt blow can be countered. Therefore, the swordsman must train to follow that technique with a proper follow-up. From (6), the attacker once again uses a men uchi attack, which is countered with the sliding block of the last example (7). As the defender (right) steps in to strike with the handle, the attacker (left) pushes his hands up to prevent the blow (8). The defender then counters this by dropping the point of his sword and cut across his opponent's midsection (9).

From (10), the attacker uses men uchi, which the defender pushes sideways (11). The defender then slams the hilt straight upward into the attacker's hands (12), so as to make an opening for a cut across the belly (13). One of the lessons learned from this type of technique is that a sword, like a human body, has several parts, and all of these parts can be used.

Often, when one begins a technique with the hand on the back of the sword, he will leave it there so as to make the countercut that much more powerful. In the days of armor, this hand could often be used to hit the back of one's own sword so as to drive it through the armor. This was particularly the case if the enemy's armor had stopped a cut and one's own sword has become lodged in the opponent's suit.

From (14), the attacker on the right uses men uchi, which is his aside (15). After the hit, the defender pushes the opponent's sword down (16), then snaps his body around to cut the neck (17). Throughout this entire sequence, the defender's hand remains on the back of his sword.

Of course, if possible, the reinforced block would counter and make a cut with the first motion. From (18), the defender sidesteps an attack and at the same time countercuts to the opponent's wrist (19). He then pushes the sword upward (20), so as to create an opening for a cut to the back of the attacker's neck (21). Once again, the defender's hand remains on the back of his sword so as to add force to the cuts.

The concept of reinforced blocks can be used against any form of attack. In the next example, the attacker in (22) makes a horizontal slash attack. The defender steps straight in and slams his sword blade into the attacker's hands (23), then shoves them upward (24) so as to cut to the belly (25).

Because the swordsmen of old Japan could never be certain when they would need their skills, it was necessary to devise techniques for a variety of situations. The next example would be a technique that would be useful at night or in other limited-light situations. The defender starts by kneeling on the ground (26), so as to better see his attacker through a "sky lighting" effect. As the attacker closes in, the defender slides to the side and cuts his wrist (27). He then stands and at the same time grabs the attacker's hand (28), so as to hold him for a countercut (29). As soon as he has struck the attacker, the defender shoves the sword across, then draws it back (30-31), to saw into the attacker's body.

1

Continued

2

3

4

5

6

7

Continued

8

9

10

11

12

13

Continued

14

15

16

17

18

19

Continued

71

20

21

22

23

24

25

Continued

26

27

28

29

30

31

Wrist Cuts

Although these are not techniques per se, the concept illustrated in these two examples are very important. Because of the razor-sharp edge of the Japanese sword, these little moves are deadly. Normally, these techniques are not written about much because they are generally used only after two swordsmen have missed with a simple attack or counter. Also, in the classical sword schools, these moves were left out of the kata the schools did in public demonstrations. While there are many forms of wrist cuts, the two examples given are probably the simplest to understand.

From (1), both swordsmen attack with cuts at the opponent's exposed elbow. This causes the two swords to clash together (2). The right swordsman then lets his sword bounce up (3), and then he brings it down to cut his opponent's wrist (4).

In the next example (5), the attacker (right) cuts at the defender's body and the defender parries (6). The attacker slides his sword down and *into* the defender's sword (7). This motion delays the defender's counter so that the attack can loop his sword into the defender's wrist from below (8).

1

2

3

4

Continued

5

6

7

8

Nito (Two Swords)

The use of two swords in Japanese fencing goes all the way back to the 16th century. Although probably not invented by any one person, this approach to fencing was made popular by the exploits of Miyamoto Musashi. Oddly enough, there is no definite proof that Musashi ever used two swords in a real duel. In fact, in more than a few of his most famous duels, he didn't even use a sword. Against Ganryu he used a boat oar, and against Baiken he used a *shuriken* (throwing knife). Against Denshichiro Yoshioka he used Denshichiro's own sword against him. Only in later life did Musashi apparently grasp the concept of two swords.

The use of two swords has many advantages. Against multiple attackers, one can present a far more complicated defense with two swords. In one-on-one situations, the second sword can be thrown to create an opening or it can make a quick attack in the same instance that a parry is made.

Often in two-sword technique, one sword is used to control the opponent's sword while the other one dispatches him. From (1), the attacker on the left uses men uchi, which is knocked aside by whipping the long sword around the defender's body (2). As the attacking sword passes harmlessly by, the defender steps forward to thrust home with the short sword (3).

The same type of concept can be used when the opponent tries to thrust between the nito man's two swords. From (4), the attacker thrusts and the defender parries with his long sword (5), then cuts the attacker's neck with his short sword (6).

Often when one counters an attack with two swords it is possible to use both swords in one motion. From (7), the attacker uses a horizontal slash. The defender steps forward and slams both his swords forward (8). One sword cuts the attacker's hands and the other checks the attacking sword. The nito man then pushes both swords up (9), and then slashes across the opponent's neck with his short sword (10).

One of the points in using the short sword in nito fashion is that of having the cut from this sword powered by the body weight as the body avoids an attack. From (11), the attacker's men uchi is sidestepped. As the defender steps he brings his short sword upward into the attacker's hands (12). If done properly, this will drive the attacker's hands upward — if it doesn't remove one or both of them entirely — (13), so that a finishing cut is possible (14).

One of the most famous nito techniques is the "X" block. In reality, this is not so much a block as a receiving form which momentarily controls the opponent's sword. From (15), the attacker uses men uchi, the defender raises both swords to form an "X" and catches the opponent's sword between them (16). The defender then pushes the swords apart. This causes the attacker's sword to move downward and at the same time frees the nito man's short sword for the final cut (17).

1

2

3

Continued

4

5

6

7

8

9

Continued

10

11

12

13

14

15

Continued

16

17

Katsijinken (Non-Killing Sword)

In spite of its deadly nature, the Japanese sword does not *have* to be used only for murder. In fact, there are many instances in the history of swordsmanship where a skillful swordsman overcame a less-skilled opponent and, at the same time, allowed the loser to live so as to learn from his lesson. The level of skill required to do this in actual application is far above that of just cutting an opponent down. Much of the skill used in the techniques or approach that one would label *katsujinken* are a direct outgrowth of an approach to kenjutsu known as *muto*, which is the ability to defeat an opponent who is armed with a sword when one is unarmed. The examples given illustrate something of this idea.

From a kneeling position, the defender awaits the attacker's move (1). The attacker uses men uchi and the defender parries by stepping up and into the attack (2). This drives the attacker's hands back and the defender strikes the attacker with an elbow to the face (3). This forces the attacker down (4), where he can be pinned (5).

Another idea often used so as to spare an opponent is mune uchi, or hitting with the back part of the blade, which in the case of the Japanese sword, is dull. From (6), the attacker on the left cuts at his opponent's head. The defender slams the back of his sword into the attacker's hands (7), and moving with the attacker's momentum, spins around (8), and throws the attacker to the ground (9), where he can be pinned (10).

Often, one can use the sword to control the opponent's sword, thus creating an opening through which he can move and grab the opponent. From (11), the attacker (left) slashes at the defender's forward hand (12). The defender adjusts his hand and lets the attack slide under his sword (13). He then pushes the attacker's sword down and using his left hand catches the opponent's sword hilt (14). By pushing upward, the defender positions the attacker (15), where a leg pin can be applied (16).

1

Continued

2

3

4

5

6

7

Continued

8

9

10

11

12

13

Continued

14

15

16

Kenjutsu and Jujutsu

As we have seen from earlier chapters, a number of different ways of using the sword were developed in Japan. These developments impacted a number of other fighting arts.

Often, weapons seemed to have been designed for litte more than countering the sword. One example is the *kusari game*, which combined the reach of a weighted chain with the speed of a small bladed weapon.

Another development, caused by a different set of circumstances, was the rise of *jujutsu*. Historically, jujutsu is really a general term that is assigned to a wide variety of martial arts which have, as a main point, the use of techniques that either do not use weapons, or employ smaller weapons which only serve to increase the pouer of the unarmed techniques.

As peace came to Japan, the need to control indivudals or small groups became more important. This created to a rise in the importance of policework, and the techniques that were once used as a back up on the battlefield became more important as the action moved from open fields to the crowded alleys of the towns. Self-defense became as much an indoor concern as a outdoor concern.

This lead to to development of combative systems that placed unarmed techniques at the center of the concept, and also placed the object of capturing an armed opponent above simple killing him. The present of weapons and several attackers was always assumed whenever practicing.

The present day state of jujutsu says much about what can happen when the context of techniques is forgotten. In many cases, the attacks used to practice jujutsu stem from the types of attack one would encounter when dressed in Japanese armor or clothing of the ancient days. Also, the enviornment has be taken into much more consideration. Such elements as lighting, number of opponent's, types of weapons present, etc., all played a part in the training of the classical jujutsuka.

A interesting aspect of jujutsu illustrated herein is the use of jujutsu techniques as they apply to the sword. Just as a person has several body parts which can be used within the martial arts, the sword has not only a blade but a scabbard, scabbard cord, handle, and many other parts that can be used within a 'fighting' situation. The fact that such techniques are rarely seen says much about how out of touch with their roots many martial arts have become. It only makes sense that if one were about to attack someone who happened to be wearing a sword (Perhaps to steal the sword!), one would try to attack in such a way as to prevent the sword from being drawn. Since this is the case, there were (and are) a number of techniques to prevent such attacks.

It should be added that the attacking techniques can also be high level and very difficult to deal with. The importance of such techniques even in today's world can be seen when one thinks that one concern of police has to be someone attempting to take their own sidearms and using them against them.

The jujutsu introduced here are from the Takagi Yoshin ryu and the Koto ryu. The Takagi ryu come from a fairly well known tradition while the Koto ryu is associated with the Iga branch of ninjutsu. Although there are better known ryu, the author has a reasonable amount of training in these two and can thus write from direct experience.

Takagi Yoshin Ryu

The curriculum of Takagi Yoshin ryu jujutsu has a number of sections. Such basic skills as breakfalls, blocks and counter-strikes, and hold releases are covered in the kihon waza. After the kihon, there are several major sections of techniques, for example, (1) Shoden No Gata (2) Chuden No Sabikigata (3) Chuden No Tai No Gata (4) Okuden No Gata (S) Eri Shimegata (6) Moguri Gata. Each of these sections has a number of lessons to offer the martial artist, and just learning the basic forms of each technique really is just the beginning.

Koto Ryu

This is the Koto ryu famous for its koppojutsu. While it has become popular to translate the Japanese "koppojutsu" as "bone breaking," the word could be applied to a wide variety of pressure point and weak-point attacks. It should be noted that nerve point attacks and weak-point attacks are not necessarily the same thing. Weak points can occur within someone's balance, stance, natural structure of body, the operation of one's individual nervous system and even the mental outlook. This confusion about what is an actual weak point as opposed to a simple sensitive spot on someone's body is one very important reason most martial artists spend their entire lives training and still reach only a rather insipid level of skill.

According to *kuden* (oral tradition), koppojutsu originated in ancient China. It is further stated that these techniques were brought to Japan by the monk Chan Busho from what is now present day Korea.

The techniques of Koto ryu are organized on the usual ancient Japanese system of Shoden, Chuden, Ikuden and Hiden. Although there is some interelationship between each level of the techniques, each group has its own important points. An interesting aspect of Koto ryu is that the techniques would work against a man dressed in wooden clothing or armor of the type worn in ancient Japan. This reflects the fact that althought the ancient ninja are often associated with the practice of spying, a number of them saw action on countless battlefields of old Japan.

The Shoden gata is contained in 18 methods. These methods deal with a variety of attacks and show the proper use of such striking techniques as kicks, head butts and different strikes with the hands. While on first examination, these techniques look fairly simple and straight forward, this is actually not the case because of the number of situations under which they can be used. It should be noted, that the Koto ryu has its oun system of attacking the various weak points of the body and the study of how to match the proper body weapon to the point that is being attacked is a rather wide area of study.

The following provides an outline of the history of the Koto ryu.The names listed are those of the headmasters of the system. There were of course, a number of famous ninja and samurai trained in the techniques of the Koto ryu. For example, the famous ninja Ishika Goemon learned Ninpo from his master Momochi Sandadu. Goemon as best remembered for his role as Japan's "Robin Hood." Goeman also attempted to kill to famed leader Hideyoshi but without success. According to popular legend, Goemon was eventually executed for his activities (as common fate for many at that time) but other Kuden states that he escaped this fate.

Koto Ryu Koppojutsu Targets:

1. Ribs under the pectoral muscle.
2. Above and below the adams apple.
3. The temple.
4. The stomach or solar plexus.
5. The groin.
6. The soft spot below the ear.
7. Under the jawline.
8. Under the collar bone near the point of the shoulder.
9. The insertion of the deltoid.
10. The separation between the bone and muscle of the upper arm.
11. The middle of the shoulder joint.
12. The bottom of the chin.
13. Under the armpit.
14. The sternum.
15. Inner ridge of the hip bone.
16. Side of the hip.
17. Ridge of the eye socket.
18. The carotid artery.
19. Base of the nose.
20. Clapping the hands over the ears.
21. The bridge of the nose.
22. The throat
23. The tissue surrounding the stomach.
24. Inner and outer thigh.
25. Just above and below the ends of the clavical.
26. The clavical.
27. The notch between the ends of the clavical.
28. Inside and outside of elbow joint.
29. Inside the shell of the cheekbone.
30. The soft spot at the top of the head.
31. The middle of the chest.
32. The ribs under the armpit.
33. The base of the thumb.
34. The ribs under the chest muscles, front and back.
35. The instep.

It should be noted that this list does not give every weak point on the body.
Takagi Yoshin ryu Photos

(1) DO GAESHI

From seiza, uki (the person receiving the technique) make a quick grab for his opponent's short sword (2). His incoming hand is caught and the other hand slams into his throat (3). This is followed by pulling back on uki's collar to force him move backwards (4). By using the front knee against the elbow, (5) reverse his motion and throw his forward onto his face (6) and then finally over the short sword.

1

2

3

4

97

5

6

(2) KATA MUNE DORI

From seiza, uki attacks with a lapel grab (7) followed by a grab at the sword handle (8). Punch directly into his grabbing hand (9). This is followed by standing and kicking to the groin (10). I then take advantage of uki's grab by catching his arm (11) and dropping on it (12).

7

8

9

10

11

12

(3) IKI CHIGAE HENKA GATA

To take another's weapon, a number of things must be taken into account. From (13) the two demonstrators pass each other. As the sword passes, the unarmed man attacks by grabbing his right hand and punching into the ribs (14). He then reachs across and grabs the sword (15) handle and uses the sword to attack uki's arm (16).

13

14

15

16

(4) HIZAGURUMA HENKA GATA

Here, the swordsman attack by drawing his sword (17) and cuts in an upward diagonal direction (18). This is countered by checking the hand and punching the elbow nerves (19). The swordsman's arm is the brought up and over (20) to create and outside wrist twist. The sword is the grabbed (21) and taken away (22).

17

18

19

20

21

22

(5) ONIKUDAKI HENKA GATA

Often, standard jujutsu techniques could be applied in a number of suprising ways. From (23) a downward cut is blocked and the sword handle is driven into the attackers stomach (24). The sword handle is the used to hook one arm into "onikudaki gata" (25). This drives the attacker's upper body down (26-27).

23

24

25

26

27

(6) DAMURA HENKA GATA

One stance that can be seen to have evolved directly from the sword wearing days is BOBI NO KAMAE (28). From this stance, a cross step is used to dodge a cut and at the same time, the scabbard is slammed into uki's wrists (29-30). This is followed by a kick to the leg (31) and a sword draw to control the situation (32).

28

29

30

31

32

(7) GOHI HENKA GATA

Defending with a short suord against a long sword (33), the draw is blocked at the wrist (34) and a blow to the elbow with the handle of the short sword (35). Finishing the draw, the fingers of the sword hand the attack the base of the throat(36). This is done by holding the sword handle loosely in the hand (37) and pushing downward (38).The technique finishs by using the sword to control uki (39-40).

33

34

35

36

37

38

39

40

(8) SOKUG0KU HENKA GATA

From bobi no kamae, (41), the downward cut is avoided by sinking to one knee and slamming the handle into uki's stomach (42). The handle is then popped into the chin (43).This is followed by a simple turn (44) into an arm bar (45).

41

42

43

44

45

Epilogue
Ittosai's Instructions

Sometime during his fiftieth year, Itto Ittosai, creator of the famed Itto ryu decided that the time had come for him to devote the rest of his life to the service of Buddha. However, before leaving the world of normal men, Itto was faced with the task of making sure that his ryu would be passed down to the next generation. Taking his two top students to a quiet field, Itto had them fight a duel to the death to decide who would be the next headmaster of the Itto ryu. The winner of the duel received Itto's sword as well as a scroll containing the secrets of Itto's style. The two students were named Zenki and Ono. During the duel, Zenki was killed and later, Ono became a tutor of the Tokugawa shoguns.

Unlike many of the sword schools in Japan that trace their origins to some divine revelation, the Itto ryu was a system that evolved directly from the experiences of its founder. Thus, it is one of the most practical of all of the old schools of Japanese swordsmanship.

For anyone interested in the older schools of Japanese fencing, the Itto ryu is both interesting and, to a certain extent, inescapable. Of course, one method of finding out a little about this school would be to visit it in Japan, but that would present some surprising drawbacks. First of all, modern kendo has made inroads into many of the old schools of fencing, and thus caused some modifications in some of the techniques. Also, the old techniques that still do exist are closely guarded and not often shown to the usual visitor. Fortunately, the scrolls left by Ittosai are still in existence and can be obtained by those who have the connections and luck.

What follows are the first parts of the instructions left by Ittosai. Here, he writes about some of the central points of swordsmanship, but the same ideas can be applied to any form of martial art. Of course, if one has some experience at sword technique, then understanding what is written here is somewhat easier.

#1 Fatsumomiska No Koto

To see depth and distance, a person needs two eyes. Whenever one looks at a person, it is not enough to just see the person's surface. One must check the entire person. The walk, the hands and the balance of the large and small points. Special points can indicate other body development. That is, what is the "unusual point" connected to (i.e., conditioned hands will reveal one type of training, while large forearms will reveal another)? In the checking technique of the Itto ryu the following points can be used:

If your opponent takes *seigan no kamae* (middle sword posture) or *gedan no kamae* (lower sword posture), then check his grip, foot position and then the entire body. Mistakes in any of these positions can tell one much about the opponent's abilities and experience.

If the opponent assumes *jodan no kamae* (upper sword posture), then check the sword edge (one indication of distance), the grip of his right hand, and the position of his elbows and then his foot and body position.

If the opponent takes *waki no kamae* (holding the sword back behind the body), then check the grip of his front hand, his footwork and his shoulder.

The point of all this is that you must be able to judge the opponent's actions based on the way he is standing (his posture). If the opponent moves to the right, check his left side; if he moves to the left, then check his right side. Always check in the opposite direction than the one in which the opponent is moving. If one cannot read an opponent's mind through his motion, then check the edge of his sword. If one still cannot read him then one must use his own sword point because the point of one's sword can scare the opponent and thus make him reveal his intentions.

The mind is the same as the true body. Even if one has a strong body but his mind is weak (because he is scared or unsure) then he is weak. If one has a weak body but a strong mind, he is strong.

One must train so he can check his own mind so that there is no weak point there (such weak points as being scared, excited, unsure or wanting to win). The object of training is to rid one's self of such weak points. However, be careful not to have an "I am strong" mind.

One needs to practice naturally. One can check an opponent through his friends, where he lives, etc. One has to keep the body and mind free and flexible. Then from one action, one can check the opponent's next action. One can find the big points through the small points.

#2 Giri Otoshi

This technique is the beginning and the end. It is easy to start but difficult to master. When the opponent cuts, then at that timing, enter and do a slide cut. This action will deflect the opponent's sword while placing one in a win position. This action is done with Aiuchi style (mutual killing style) but because of the timing, one wins. Thus with proper timing, one steps straight in and cuts straight down.

To do this, one must have *mushin* (no mind) because no power is used. This works because one's mind is already in a winning position. That is, one's own mind balance is best while the opponents' mind balance is totally broken. To create a winning position like this, one must be able to cut without thinking. Thus, as the opponent cuts, one's own mind is patient in that one does not *want* to cut the opponent. That is, there is no desire to win. If one is worried or wants to win, then the mind is fixed, and he will not be able to move freely. With mushin, it is easy to check the opponent. For example, if a cat is chasing a mouse too closely, sometimes the mouse will turn and attack, and the cat will have a difficult time in spite of the mouse's small size. However, a good cat will keep a "play" mind and catch the mouse very easily. This type of mind leads to a happy and lucky lifestyle. If one masters Giri Otoshi, then a nice, dignified style will be born. This technique is like a seed dropped onto the ground that will grow and develop into countless techniques.

#3 Inken No Koto

In real fighting, the opponent wants to get close enough to win. This is the case for both fighters. Even if the distance is equal, but one side can attack with ease while the other cannot, the true distance is not equal. This is the situation one must study and learn to create. The most important point is to keep the body straight and use footwork to adjust one's distance. One should learn how to make the opponent feel like he is always far away, and thus cannot attack. If the true distance is close for both people, then change position to gain the advantage.

One must keep flexible in the approach to be able to do this. If the true distance is close then it is also possible to use a mind attack. This is done to create distance in the opponent so that even though the physical distance is the same, the mind distance is not. That is, the mind relationship is changed. The decision of life or death balances on very small points. One can use devices (i.e., tricks or other techniques) to break the opponent's balance (mental balance). If one thinks too much or is too scared or too concerned with winning, then he will not be able to find correct technique.

#4 Yoko Tati Joge Koto

If your opponent cuts at your body (*do giri*) then go straight in or straight out. If he cuts downward at your head (*shomen uchi*), cut straight upward. Use the opposite direction technique for an easy victory.

This is the basic idea, but techniques are not fixed. One can break the opponent's balance by using his power against him and this brings an easy win. It is important not to let the opponent control your mind or body, so keep your own rhythm and pace.

The point is to make a scale like a ball and only as one starts actions. That is, cut with the sword directly from where it is. If it is high, cut down, and if low, cut up. Don't move your sword around needlessly. In the Itto ryu, a cut from the side (*do giri*) is *katsujinken* (life giving), while a downward cut (*shomen uchi*) is a killing technique.

One must cut one's own ego before he can use this technique. One should have a relaxed mind and keep practicing. One's own life and death depend on flexible self-control.

#5 Eroski No Koto

If something is in a shadow, then one cannot see what it truly is. That is, the truth is hidden. Often, one's opponent's mind is like this. If one can find the opponent's mind and take it (control it), then victory will be easy. Before one can do this, he must be able to find the opponent's true mind and not be taken in by outside (surface) appearances. One can combine the mind with the sword point, and with these together, break the opponent's balance and win. One's own state of mind must dictate the opponent's state of mind (i.e., make one's own pace). Often, surface appearances can cause confusion, so one must look past these to see the opponent's true mind. It is important to remember that sometimes highly skilled opponents cannot be controlled.

#6 Migokuro No Koto

The mind gathers and can be checked through the eyes. When the mind moves, it will start an eye action. Thus, reactions can be seen in the movements of the eyes. This idea can be used in fighting. For example, distractions can be used to move someone's mind. This point should be studied. Here the starting point is the mind and then, a little later, the eye moves. If one will check the eyes along with the opponent's actions, he can see his opponent's true mind.

This check should be done in one action, then one can do the techniques without thinking. Look to see where the opponent's mind is. Is it in his hands or his feet or his eye, etc.? If his mind is in his hands, maybe he is afraid. Sometimes his mind will gather in his feet. If one learns how to se where the opponent's mind is, then after this training he can fight in the dark by feeling.

If one's own eye is strong (can see the opponent's mind, etc.), then through just one action (of the opponent) one can read everything about him. This is why an old teacher can defeat a young and very strong student; the teacher's eye is stronger. This type of strong eye can be used to contact God.

#7 Kogishin No Koto

A fox can run very fast to escape. However, if a dog attacks him and the fox thinks too much about how to escape, he will not escape. Don't use too much thinking. Too much thinking can cause doubt, and this is a problem. If one's own mind is confused like this, then he will not be able to see the opponent's mind and cannot use the technique. If one has doubt in the technique, then the technique will be useless. One gets rid of this by practice and experience. When teaching, one must be careful with the voice because the student will believe.

#8 Shofu No Koto

A pine tree has no voice. The wind by itself also has no voice. Together, they have a sound. As the wind blows fast or slow through the pines, it makes different sounds. Wind from the south has a different sound than a wind from the north, and these are different from the sound of the winds in the mountains or by the seashore.

It is the same against an opponent. If he changes his style, then adapt. To always have the same style is not good. If one's opponent has a strong style, use a stronger style. If the opponent has a weak style, then use an even weaker style. This is one type of approach.

Another approach is to use weakness when the opponent is strong and use strength when the opponent is weak. These two approaches are very important.

If one's opponent is too strong, then confuse his mind with timing, tricks, etc. It is most important that one know his own points (strong and weak) or he will have problems. With the wind and the pine trees, if one is missing then there is no sound. If one's opponent has a fighting mind while one does not, then there will be no trouble (dealing with the situation).

#9 Chika No Koto

There are many ground conditions one must be aware of. Sometimes one will meet the opponent on flat ground and sometimes on hilly ground and sometimes on rocky or muddy ground. In addition to these conditions, there are the conditions that one finds in a house or castle. One must learn to always make the best of the situation. If one's actions fit the ground they are on, then the entire technique will be much easier.

In all situations, one should keep the body straight and let the feet and legs adapt to the ground. If one is on slippery ground (i.e., ice or wet ground), then one should use a narrow step (small steps). If one finds obstacles on the ground, such as stones, then use a sliding step because using a high step to step over things can cause one to lose balance. If possible, have sunlight to one's back or right. If one faces many attackers, then put one's back to a wall or other cover.

#10 Mutashinsu No Koto

This is divided into three steps:

(1) Study one thing (the Itto ryu) well. Once one has done this, he can look at other martial arts and adapt them so they are useful to himself. Thus, one can look at other activities through he art. Look through Itto ryu eye. It should be remembered that different activities have different key points that should be checked.

(2) If one can't find the opponent's mind, he should not attack because one cannot win like this. One must feel the opponent's mind. This is the basis of the Itto ryu.

(3) If one's practice has reached a point where he almost completely understands the Itto ryu, then the opponent will not be able to read his mind. Thus, the opponent is always confused and cannot attack. This makes the opponent weak and afraid and breaks him. As one's practice increases (the amount of time practiced) then he will realize and easy, natural understanding. The personality will grow and he will naturally fit into whatever situation he is in. The mind will not be influenced by the outside world and will always be quiet (inside). This is one high target for the mind practice.

#11 Mai No Koto

One starts hitting or thrusting with the posture (stance). One should finish techniques without using much power. The best distance is not too close or too far. It is a "best fit distance." This is one type of *mai* (distance). One must always use this distance for real fighting. This fit is different for each person.

In the Itto ryu, the distance between one's own feet when standing in a stance is about 90 cm. The distance between people (between oneself and the opponent) is about six feet. At a distance of 150 cm between each person, the fight is won or lost if one has the best principle. Winning starts when one has the best distance and the opponent does not.

A highly skilled technician always makes the best distance while a low-skilled person cannot. Sword techniques, such as hitting the opponent's sword, etc., are all meant to create this best distance so one can go inside the opponent's guard and attack. When one walks on the street, he should check his distance from other people and create the best distance as a way of practice. When one visits a house, he should mind the distance between him and the host.

Mind distance is also important. In a fighting situation, if one's own mind is sharp, then he may "draw out" the opponent's attack. One should not think "want life" thoughts when faced with a real fight. One should take the attitude of *Shin No Shin Ken*, which means one will not stop even if cut. If one has proper mind distance but technique is not there, he cannot win. One must have both technique and mind distance.

#12 Zanshin No Koto

(1) One should only use 88 percent of the mind and body power when doing a technique. If one uses full power, then the next technique is lost. For example, one never cooks 100 percent of the rice because then there is nothing left for the next year if the crops are bad. One should save 12 percent, but at the same time give 88 percent fully and at one time.

(2) Mind in technique: If one uses 100 percent of the mind in a technique, then the mind becomes fixed. Mind and body should be used completely together only in the very best situations (for example, when the opponent's mind and body balance are totally broken). However, remember that if one does not put enough mind into a technique then it will be easy to counter. Study this balance.

(3) If one does use 100 percent mind and body in a technique, then he should use another principle so as to always have another technique beyond the last. *Zanshin* is a last caution.

Notes

Notes

Notes

Notes

Notes